What to Do About Woolsey?

Jennifer Jiménez
Illustrated by Judy Love

Rigby®

A Harcourt Achieve Imprint

www.Rigby.com
1-800-531-5015

This is Jessie.
This is Jessie's lamb, Woolsey.
Jessie and Woolsey are best friends.
They do everything together.

Woolsey is always there when Jessie needs him.
He's even there when Jessie gets sick
and has to visit the doctor.

One day Jessie saw his friend David at school.

"Hi, Jessie," said David.
"Can you come to my birthday
sleepover on Friday?

"I'll ask my mom," Jessie answered.

5

Jessie was very excited.
He had been asked to go to his first sleepover!
Then Jessie thought about Woolsey.
Should he take Woolsey to the party?

Jessie's mom said he could go to the party.
Jessie thought about the sleepover all week.
He still didn't know what to do about Woolsey.

On Friday Jessie packed pajamas,
a toothbrush, toothpaste, and a comb.
He did not pack Woolsey.

Jessie knew he would miss Woolsey.
However, he was afraid the other boys
would laugh if he brought his lamb.
Jessie wasn't sure what to do.

"Mom," called Jessie, "what should I do about Woolsey?"

She said, "Why couldn't you take Woolsey, and just keep him in your backpack?"

"That's a good idea," said Jessie.

Jessie's mom and dad took him to David's house.

"Hi!" said David. "Come in and meet my friends.
This is Connor, Jabari, and Emerson."

The boys had a lot of fun,
and Jessie slept without Woolsey
for the first time.

When his mom picked him up,
he grabbed his backpack, ran to the car,
and told her about the party.

Jessie got home and opened the backpack.
He found a green dinosaur!
Where was Woolsey?
Jessie realized that he had taken Emerson's
backpack by mistake!

Jessie saw Emerson at school on Monday morning.

"I have your backpack," said Jessie,
"and your dinosaur."

"And I have your backpack," said Emerson,
"and your lamb."

"What's your lamb's name?" Emerson asked.

"Woolsey," Jessie answered.
"What's your dinosaur's name?"

"Dino," said Emerson.

"Cool," said Jessie.
"Let's eat lunch together today!"

"Sure!" said Emerson.

Jessie and Emerson became best friends.

Woolsey and Dino didn't go
to any more sleepovers.